For my Amma and Achan though whom I felt the love of God.

Contents

SEETHING CAULDRONS IN MAHESH DATTANI'S PLAYS

A CRITICAL STUDY TAARA AND FINAL SOLUTIONS

DR. ANUJA RAJ

ISBN 978-1-68487-188-9

Preface

Dattani and his plays are widely acclaimed in the current scenario. He can be notably called as a master of social themes when it comes to equipping his plays. The current book is one among the many varied set of study that can be done in parse his plays. the academia needs more study on these kind of works and apply current theoretical studies into this matter. The title Seething Cauldrons has been used to justify the ignited themes that the playwright kindles in his plays. These fires still burn fresh within the Indian context.

Acknowledgements

My sincere gratitude to my PG Research Guide and Supervisor, Dr. Sandhya P. Pai, Associate Professor and Former Head (Rtd.), Department of English, St. Joseph's College for Women, Alappuzha, who showed infinite patience and understanding in addition to her usual skill in scrutinizing, correcting and editing the manuscript and the draft. I am ever indebted to her for her support and help.

I would also like to acknowledge the sincere support and unfailing help rendered to me by Prof. Tessy Xavier, Head of the Department of English. She has always been a constant source of inspiration and encouragement in all my intellectual activities.

I also use this opportunity to express my sincere gratitude to the Principal and staff members who served as an inspiration during my period of study.

I would also like to express my gratitude to the librarians of the University Library and the Public Library, Paravoor, without forgetting the staff of the college library for their infinite patience and support in helping me to hunt for books.

I would also like to acknowledge the support of my parents and my husband Mr. Shinu Chandran in helping me to complete this project.

Dr. Anuja Raj.

CHAPTER ONE

Introduction

Drama still remains the 'sad Cinderella of Indian English Literature' waiting for her prince charming. Beginning with K.N. Banergee's *The Persecuted* (1831), it has emerged with more than five hundred plays to its credit. Still it is relegated to the third position in Indian Literature in English after fiction and poetry. Very few playwrights writing in English have established their credentials as dramatists. Asif Currimbhoy and Mahesh Dattani stand at the top. Mahesh Dattani is the foremost Indian playwright writing in English today.

India has the longest and the richest tradition in Drama. Origin of Indian Drama can be traced to the ancient rituals and seasonal festivities of the Vedic Aryans which were crude and closely connected to their life experience. Later, as drama evolved, different episodes from the myths and legends based on the *Ramayana*, the *Mahabharata* and the *Bhagavatha* were picked up and enacted out in front of the people. This kind of a performance is still very popular in India especially during Dussehra when the episode of the killing of Ravana is enacted.

There are references to drama in Patanjali's *Vyakarna Mahabhashya*, Jain's *Aagam of Raypaseni Sutta* as well as Vatsyayan's *Kamasutra*, Kautilya's *Arthasastra* and Panini's

Ashtadhyai. Thus the origin of Sanskrit Drama dates back to 1000 BC. Bharata's *Natyasastra* is the most significant work on Indian dance and drama. Besides everything about composition, production, and enjoyment of ancient drama, a wealth of information about types of plays, dress, stage equipment, production and music is also dealt with in detail. The *Natyasasthra* is considered to be the fifth Veda, drawing the quintessence of drama out of the four Vedas: dance from the *Rig Veda*, song from the *Sama Veda*, mimicry from *Yajur Veda* and passion from *Atharva*, and Bharata is regarded as the deity of the Indian theatre.

Bharata ascribed a divine origin to drama. Its origin seems to be from religious dancing. According to Bharata, poetry (kavya), dance (nritta), and mime (nritya) in life's play (leela) produce emotion (bhava) but only drama (natya) produces flavour (rasa). The drama uses the eight basic emotions of love, joy (humour), anger, sadness, pride, fear, aversion and wonder attempting to resolve them in the ninth holistic feeling of peace. Bharata Muni summarises his dramatic theory thus "The combination called Natya is a mixture of rasa, bhavas, abhinayas, dharmis, vrittis, pravrittis, siddhi, svaras, instruments, song and theatre-house" (*Dramatic Concepts, Greek and Indian*, 86). The most renowned and talented dramatists of the ancient era are Ashwaghosha, Bhasa, Shudraka, Kalidasa, Harsha, Bhavabhuti, Vishakhadatta, Bhattanarayana, Murari and Rajashekhara.

Till the fifteenth century, plays of Sanskrit tradition were performed on stage in Tamil Nadu, Kerala, Karnataka, Andhra, Uttar Pradesh, and Gujarat. Sanskrit dramas were staged approximately up to the fifteenth century, but thereafter, Indian dramatic activity almost ceased due to foreign invasion of India.

The beginnings of Loknatya (People's Theatre) are noticed in every state of India from the seventeenth century onwards. We see in Bengal 'Yatrakirtaniya' (known as *Jathra*),'Paal' and 'Gaan'; in Madhya Pradesh 'Mach', in Kashmir 'Bhandyathaar' while in Gujarat the forms were 'Bhavai', 'Ramleela' and 'Rasleela'; in Maharashtra 'Tamasha', in Rajasthan 'Raas' and 'Jhoomer'; in Punjab 'Bhangra' and 'Song'; and in Assam it was 'Abhiyanat' and 'Ankinatya'; in Bihar it was 'Videshiya'; and 'Chhau' in West Bengal and Bihar. The people living in Southern India began presenting the plays in their Devasthanas in their ancient traditional forms with accompaniment of music and dance called 'Bhagvatmela,' 'Yakshgana' and 'Kudiyattam'.

The rise of the modern Indian drama dates back to the eighteenth century when the British Empire consolidated its stable power in India. In 1765 one Russian drama lover Horasin Lebedef and Bengali drama lover Gulokhnath had staged two English comedies *Disgaij* and *Love is the Best Doctor*. But the real beginning was in 1831 when Prasanna Kumar Thakur established the 'Hindu Rangmanch' at Calcutta and staged Wilson's English translation of Bhavabhuti's Sanskrit drama *Uttar Ramacharitam*. Social drama of Girish Chandra Ghosh, historical dramas of D.L. Roy and artistic dramas of Rabindranath Tagore (*Mukta Dhara, Chandalika*) were staged in the theatres during the period of the worst-ever famines of Bengal and the Second World War. The staging of these realistic plays marked the beginning of the Parallel Theatre. Modern or Parallel Theatre is a more realistic reflection of the existing Indian environment. Performed in a host of regional languages, Parallel Theatre is projected in several styles and techniques.

Closely following the trends of Bengali theatre, theatres of Marathi, Kannada, Gujarati, Oriya and Hindi were also developing. In the middle of the nineteenth century Indian theatre was equally influenced by the western literature and the feeling of nationalism and pride in the glorious past of the country. In 1852-1853, the famous Parsi Theatre was launched in Bombay which influenced the whole country in no time. Postaji Pharmji was the pioneer in establishing the Parsi theatre company in India. Many new theatre experiences were brought up on stage during Parsi theatre's evolution in India. On the other hand, the amateur theatre also developed with Bharatendu Harishchandra (*A History of Indian English Drama* 3).

Indian theatre and drama got a new footing when Kendriya Sangeet Natak Akademi was started in January 1953. Institutions like 'Anamika' in Calcutta(1955), Theatre Unit in Bombay (1954) and Three Arts Club (1948), Little Theatre Group (1951), Independence Theatre (1959) also played a great role in establishing the modern Indian theatre. State academies were also set up in the most of the states in 1950s. However, the most important development was the starting of the National School of Drama at New Delhi, set up by the Sangeet Natak Akademi in 1959.

In the 1960s by suitable mixing of various styles and techniques from Sanskrit, medieval folk and western theatre, the modern Indian theatre was given a new versatile and broader approach at every level of creativity. Slowly, many writers broke the barriers of regional languages and produced many good works at the national level. Badal Sircar, Girish Karnad (*Hayavadana [1975]*, *Nagamandala [1990]*), Vijay Tendulkar, Mohan Rakesh (*Aadhe-Adhure, Aashaad ka Ek Din*), Adya Rangacharya and

Dharamveer Bharati (*Swarg our Prithvi, Saans ki Kalam se*) are the few among them.

The year 1972 was a landmark year for Indian vernacular theatre, Vijay Tendulkar's Marathi play *Ghashiram Kotwal* made waves by its brilliant use of "Tamasha" folk form of Maharashtra in modern contemporary theatre. This led to the birth of a new breed of directors like B.V. Karanth, HabibTanveer, Bansi Kaul and Rattan Thiyyam. Recently 'Dishantar' group of Om Shivpuri and 'Abhiyan' of RajinderNath have staged many notable dramas which will be remembered for long. In recent years the country has also produced talented playwrights who have chosen English as their medium. Indian English plays like Gurcharan Das's *Mira*, Partap Sharma's *A Touch of Brightness* and Asif Currimbhoy's*The Dumb Dancer*, have been staged in the west. Younger writers like Mahesh Dattani and Manjula Padmanabhan have infused new life into this branch of writing. Padmanabhan's Onassis award-winning *Harvest* has achieved worldwide acclaim. Incidentally, both Dattani and Padmanabhan write about mean, ugly, unhappy things of life; Padmanabhan projects a dehumanized, terrifying world in which mothers sell their sons for the price of rice. Padmanabhan projects in her play a more serious, grim and unpalatable world than Dattani. The plays of Dattani have been quite successful on the stage and have captured the imagination of the middle class audience. Dattani has the honour of being the first Indian English playwright to win the Sahitya Akademi Award – the highest literary award of the country – in 1998, for his most sensitive and the only political play *Final Solutions*.

Dattani's *Final Solutions and Other Plays* (1994) consists of four full-length plays. These are – *Where There's a Will*,

Dance Like a Man, Bravely Fought the Queen, and Final Solutions. The second collection, *Collected Plays* was published in 2000. It has six full length plays and two radio plays. These are – *Where There's a Will, Dance Like a Man, Tara, Bravely Fought the Queen* and *Final Solutions* and *On a Muggy Night in Mumbai.* The two radio plays are – *Do the Needful* and *Seven Steps around the Fire.*

Mahesh Dattani is primarily concerned with the problems of common man. Sometimes he discusses unconventional subjects also. This he has done in his *Dance Like a Man*, where "the protagonists Jairaj takes to dancing, against the express wishes of his father, also marries a dancer". He has dramatized homosexuality, a taboo for an Indian, in *A Muggy Night in Mumbai.* He is the first Indian English playwright to deal with this theme. Dattani is preoccupied with social and political realities in India today. His themes include Indian joint family and its impact on the individual; the plight of woman in Indian society; and homosexuality – an explosive subject (for an Indian).

Where There's a Will discusses the negative effect of parent's love for their children. There are three characters in the play, who are the victims of negative influence of love in their own way. Hashmukh Mehta has to live his entire life under the strict observance of his father. He expects his son Ajit to do the same. Hashmukh's wife, Sonal, realizes very late that she also was under the shadow of her elder sister, Minal. She is much pained to say, "Even at my husband's funeral, she sat beside me and told me when to cry" (*Collected Plays* 186). She becomes vocal to save herself before it is too late and asks her sister "Go, jump into a bottomless pit" (193).

Dance Like a Man is about an unconventional theme. The protagonist, Jairaj, chooses to become a dancer. His father does not like his decision but he does not care for his father's wish. To make matters worse he marries a dancer. His decision costs him his house. He has to struggle hard for his livelihood. He restores his self-respect by demolishing the rose-garden of his father. This is what he does first after inheriting his late father's property. He just wants to get rid of all the memories of his father. As the rose-garden was dear to his father, it was the first to be demolished. The play depicts the clash of generations having different attitudes to dance as career. The play also discusses the social prejudice against the art of dance and the plight of temple-dancers.

Tara tells us the story of Siamese twins conjoined at the waist. The main characters in the play are Tara and Chandan. They are victims of social prejudices. Tara is denied of her right leg just for the sake of Chandan. Chandan's body rejects the leg and both of them have to depend on the artificial legs. Bharati, the mother suffers from guilt-complex and dies ultimately of nervous breakdown. Patel, the father, suffers in his own way. He repents for his confusion and helplessness to prevent the operation, which was performed to favour Chandan at the cost of Tara. The play is about the role of family and shows what happens when in-laws interfere. It also throws light on the materialistic approach of medical professionals.

Bravely Fought the Queen is based on the story of Laxmibai, the Rani of Jhansi. Her name is invoked as an ironic parallel to the women in the play who are passive, helpless victims of male tyranny. There are three women, victimized in their own way. Old Baa is neglected by her sons and daughter-in-law. Her elder daughter-in-law, Dolly is a victim of her husband's brutality and she has a handicapped daughter. Her second daughter-in-law has a homosexual husband. Baa's sons are a failure in business.

On a Muggy Night in Mumbai is about the problem of homosexuality. The play presents a group of well-to-do homosexuals in Bombay, their changing mutual relationships, their revelations, their self-delusions and self-discoveries.

Final Solutions is Dattani's only political play. This play brought him the most coveted Sahitya Akademi Award. It discusses what happens when distrust and hatred guide members of different communities living in society. It describes how innocent people become victims of communal frenzy and postulates that "if we understand and believe in one another, nothing can be destroyed."(241). Familial relationship has also been dealt with in this play. Hardika's hatred of her in-laws as they persecuted her and Smita's love for Babban, a hopeless passion, are some of the problems discussed in the play.

Do the Needful is Dattani's radio play. He has discussed an unconventional theme along with his usual theme, family relationships. The story revolves round the two families looking for bride and bridegroom for their son and daughter. Patel is a Gujarati businessman. Gowda is a wealthy Mysorean. The two families could get the marriage solemnized with much effort. But the marriage did not work. Lata runs away to her lover the day she knows that her husband is a homosexual.

Seven Steps Around the Fire also deals with an equally explosive theme. Partly a detective play, it revolves around the mystery surrounding the murder of a hijra. To add more spice to the mystery is the hijra's being married to a minister's son. The play provides an extensive study into the lives of the hijras and the customs they follow and the beliefs they have.

30 Days in September is a depiction of the trauma that the survivors of child sexual abuse go through. The play is about the painful experience of a mother and her child who have been the victims of child abuse in their childhood. Dattani's *Mad About Money* is about gender conflict. But it's actually an updated version of his first play, *Where There is a Will.*

Mahesh Dattani's plays have aroused a wide critical interest. Many journal articles have been written about individual plays, but book length studies are by far, few. A dissertation titled *The Construction of Contemporary Indian Subjectivity in the Selected Plays of Vijay Tendulkar, GirishKarnad and Mahesh Dattani,* critically examines the concept of subjectivity in the plays of the three stalwarts of contemporary Indian drama. *Critical Response to Mahesh Dattani,* a collection of journal articles is in the process of being compiled.

The dissertation titled *Seething Cauldrons: A study of the thematic concerns in the plays of Mahesh Dattani,* undertakes to analyze Dattani's two preeminent plays, *Tara* and *Final Solutions* thematically by probing into the central issues upheld in each play. While *Tara* highlights the issue of Gender discrimination, *Final Solutions* undertakes to question the issue of communalism. In Chapter II of the thesis, titled *Tara: Issues of Gender Discrimination,* the play is analyzed in depth showing how Dattani has foregrounded this issue through the portrayal of his characters. *Chapter III Final Solutions: Issue of Communalism* delves into the ravages of communalist actions and bend of mind in the psyche of the characters. Chapter IV Conclusion sums up the findings of the thesis.

CHAPTER TWO

Tara: Issues of Gender Discrimination

Dattani's *Tara* is a riveting play that questions the role of a society that treats the children of the same womb in two different ways. It is a poignant play about a boy and a girl who are joined together at the hip and have to be separated surgically, which will mean the death of either of the two. The fact that the injustice perpetuated by the victim's own mother whose preference is to the male child, makes the play more powerful suggesting that it is woman who continues the chain of injustice. *Tara* is not just the story of the protagonist of the play 'Tara,' but it is the story of every girl child born in Indian family whether urban or rural. The situation is aggravated if the girl is physically challenged or there is any other physical or mental deformity in her. It is a bitter example of child abuse present in the Indian societies. Every girl child born in an Indian family does suffer some kind of exploitation and if there is a boy child in the family, the exploitation is very much visible as the privileges are consciously or unconsciously propounded to the son. The scene opens in London with Chandan, now a playwright, reminiscing about his childhood days spent with his sister Tara. Tara and Chandan are two sides of the same self rather than two separate entities and that Dan, the name assumed by Chandan in his later life, in trying to write the story of his own childhood, has to write Tara's story. The play revolves around the Siamese twins, Chandan and Tara. An operation to separate the twins at birth, leaves Tara crippled for life. Chandan, the privileged brother wants to turn his anguish into drama on his sister's childhood. Throughout the play we can feel that she bears some kind of grudge against the society. She seems to have some kind of aversion with the outside world and her world consists of only her parents and her brother whom she was ever close to. The play explores besides exposing the typical Indian mind set which has from time immemorial preferred a boy child to a girl child. It looks at the triumphs and the failures of an Indian family, comprising of father (Patel), mother (Bharati) and two children (Chandan and Tara) coping with the trauma of disability. Tara, a feisty girl, who isn't given enough opportunities as were given to her brother, eventually wastes away and dies. Chandan escapes to London, changes his name to Dan and attempts to repress the guilt he feels over his sister's death. His sense of trauma and anguish is so intense that at the end of the play, we see Chandan apologizing to Tara in the most moving of all the lines "Forgive me, Tara, forgive me, for making it my tragedy" (371).

Mahesh Dattani is the spokesperson of all the marginalized people. "Every individual," he says, "wants to be part of society, of the mainstream but we must acknowledge that it is a forced harmony" (The Plays of MaheshDattani, 35). His plays are played out on multi-level sets where interior and exterior become one, and geographical locations collapse – in short, his settings are as fragmented as the families who inhabit them.

The identity crisis of women in *Tara* is a topic for analysis. Tara is an ideal character of Dattani which has been widely applauded and variedly interpreted. Dattani himself has tried to depict male-dominated world. No matter how much the world proclaims about woman enfranchisement and feminine liberation, subconsciously all women are aware of the fact that they have to go a long way to break the shackles.

Tara gives us a glimpse into the modern society which claims to be liberal and advanced in its thought and action. It is therefore evident enough to confirm male chauvinism prevalent in the present society. The society which claims giving equality to women differentiates between a male child and female child. All the propagandas of equality between male and female, equal opportunities to women in all the fields are belied. Dattani has attempted an uphill task of pulling out all the taboo subjects from under the rug and putting them on the stage for the public to review.

Dattani's *Tara* gives us a picture of the helplessness of woman in our society. It has received great applause in foreign countries where students have pointed out Tara and Chandan as two aspects of same personality. As Chandan exists, by writing about himself, he writes about Tara to rediscover the neglected half of himself. But Dattani's aim in writing the play was to highlight the preference given to a male child over a female child. Whenever the question of choice comes between male and female, it is the male who is chosen.

The play *Tara* also brings forth the bizarre reality of the woman playing second fiddle to man. It opens with Chandan changed into Dan in order to absolve himself from the guilt of killing his sister. Though the poor soul had nothing to do with his sister's untimely death but he bears the brunt of his grandfather's and mother's cruelty. He feels someway responsible for his sister's death and decides to atone for it. For that reason, he escapes to London and transforms his name from Chandan to Dan and lives a self-condemned life. The viciousness of the grandfather and his mother not only takes away the life of the girl but also ruins the life of the boy who was very much attached to his sister Tara.

The fateful leg which was the cause of Tara's bad health and consequent death could not be given to the boy as it became useless after few days. The leg would have been complete success with Tara's body. It would not only have saved her life but also made her a complete person which she very much desired to be, more than Chandan. Chandan was more complacent with his handicapped life while Tara craved every moment for a complete and normal life. The awareness that she has a handicap and the humiliation meted out to her by Roopa and her friends when she was forced to show her handicapped leg to them was like a dagger-jibe to her heart.

The preference for the beneficence of the male child while staking the life of the female child is pathetic and takes to culmination the feeling of rejection felt by women in our society. So much for the educational policies framed out for the literacy of the women folk and the society as a whole, after self-reliance attained by many women in almost all the fields, if such differentiation is done as in Mahesh Dattani's *Tara*, all the declarations and proclamations seem useless.

Patel and Bharati are educated parents and the step taken by them is lamentable. Bharati's father, a resourceful person, is also considered to be one of the factors in this mishap. If Bharati had been led astray by her father's high-handed decision, why didn't Patel stand against their decision? The incompatibility, which comes between Patel and Bharati after this operation and its futility, tolls heavily on their later life which becomes full of bickering and showdowns.

Having proved wrong in her decision on the fateful 'leg', Bharati tries to shed her burden of guilt by showing maternal love and concern for her daughter and to assert her moral superiority over her husband. She also tries to expiate by the act of donating kidney to her daughter which was ultimately futile. Patel on the other hand has no compunction for being party to the wrong decision, thanks to gender patriarchy. He tries to accommodate his son Chandan and plans out his education and career for him.

At one point when Tara refuses to fill forms for college and Chandan does likewise, Patel wants Tara to comply not for her own sake but for the sake of her brother. Patel seems to have ruled out the pangs of guilt from his heart of complicity in the injustice done towards Tara. Tara being a girl has been taken for granted by Patel and all his expectations and dreams rest on Chandan whereas Chandan has been shown as a boy of a different mentality. When he finally comes to know about the injustice done towards Tara by their parents and grandfather, he is filled with self-guilt and takes up the burden solely on his own shoulder so much so that he leaves India and escapes to London under the name of Dan. Even today, the girls, most of the time, have to submit to the desires of their parents to see their brothers comfortable settled. The sons may be less talented and less intelligent than their daughters, but parents prefer spending money on sons for they believe that the sons are such assets which would stay with them while the girls would go away to their in-laws. Therefore money spent on girls would prove an unnecessary drain on the purse.

Ours has been a patriarchal society where men have always enjoyed a privileged position. Dattani has cleverly exploited this aspect which still remains like a pockmark on the face of our society.

Tara was more enthusiastic and full of zest and spark of life. She had high aspirations which she could not accomplish because of her handicapped state while the boy was comfortably located and had come to terms with his handicapped life. The question raised is why Tara was denied the privilege of the good 'leg'. It would have remained workable if attached to Tara's body. Its severance not only made Tara handicapped but also endangered her life and consequently she died an early death. Was it because she was a girl? Is being a girl in this society a curse? But do not upholders of the society realize the fact that without girls and consequently women, the society will ultimately come to a standstill? As it is, the ratio of women compared to men is much less in our country, and many such pertinent questions emerge out.

Like men, women need space to breathe freely and flourish. Mahesh Dattani has tried to show this by bringing in Dr. Thakkar as a social element with the play. Doctors are thought to be messengers of God because they save lives on this earth. Sometimes, when ordinary human beings falter, it is the doctors who show them the right path. Female foeticide has become very common. People have degraded themselves to such an extent that they kill the foetus of the female child even before it takes shape in the uterus.

In this play, Dr. Thakkar belied his godly profession and led himself to be bribed by Bharati's father into becoming an accomplice in the bizarre act of severing the leg. He should have upheld his profession by denouncing the decision at its inception whereas he in a way took Tara's life by severing the leg. His wise decision could have given Tara a safe, secured and complete life. His cruelty not only thwarts Tara's dreams but fills her life with dejection and depression. Her depression made her wish for death than unnecessarily spend money on herself. She also started hating all males including Chandan and Patel. One person she cared for was her mother. Her father's attitude toward their mother filled her with distaste for her father and on one occasion she told Chandan that their father was denying her access to their mother. When Tara comes to know about the complicity of her father, mother and grandfather in denying her a full and happy life, she is devastated and Chandan is filled with self-guilt. He is ashamed of what his parents and grandfather did to Tara. Both turn to each other for support and are shown clinging to each other at the end of the play.

Though this is a play about the injustices done to women, it is also a play about injustice to men such as Chandan. For no fault of his own, he is forced to lead a life of guilt. He could not forgive himself for the atrocity done towards his sister. He considers himself responsible for his sister's death which resulted into his refuge in London. When his father informed him about his mother's death, he refused to come back to India.

Identity crisis is strident in our society. Tara is sacrificed because she was a girl and had no right to have a better life than her brother. The idea of a complete girl-child and an incomplete male-child is so shocking that sacrifice of the girl-child is acceptable than a handicapped male-child. Then the revelation of the futility of the decision is taken with so much coolness that no compunction is shown towards the injustice done to the female child.

In case of Dattani's *Tara* too, Bharati's father who was senior-most of the three and a powerful and rich politician, was the person who determined about the operation in which the leg was to be given to Chandan instead of Tara. He went as far as bribing the doctor with sanction of land in Bangalore. Dr. Thakkar fell from his high position and without giving a second thought, along with his team, instead of taking a sound medical decision of leaving the leg with Tara, sold out his conscience for his ambitions and the temptation, to people, who had decided on the basis of gender and not on medical grounds.

Bharati's father further strengthened his indulgence for male grandchild by leaving his property after his demise to Chandan and not a single penny to Tara. He has been a consistent upholder of values pertaining to males. Patel's attitude has also been negative. He remained a mute observer of the whole affair. Isn't it because he too subscribes to the ideology of the patriarchal world? He blames his wife and father-in-law for the damage done but his complicity in the whole operation cannot be denied.

The fact that the male is always given the greater chance is obvious from Patel's planning for Chandan's education and future career. Bharati started fawning over Tara because of her sense of guilt but Patel doesn't seem to have cared much about it. It is more of gender patriarchy which dominates the play to underline which Dattani makes Dan apologize to Tara at the end of the play: "Forgive me Tara. Forgive me for making it my tragedy" (371).

After the injustice done, the deficiency is tried to be patched up by love. Bharati uses her love for Tara as a weapon against Patel as well as an expression of her desire to compensate to Tara. Female-children are more sensitive than male-children. Tara is also taken up by her mother's concern and indulgence of her; little did she know that her loving mother was an accomplice in destroying her dreams. Bharati's unnecessary bullying of Roopa into friendship with Tara and trying to bribe her into spending more time with Tara is disgusting and demeaning.

Tara is neither Chandan's tragedy not is it really Tara's. The tragic events depicted in the play are the tragic action belonging to everyday life. It is Dattani's world where the playwright picks up various characters from the society as puppets, makes society the background and displays to us the fiery issues of today. In this play, Dattani became a juggler and juggles with husband and wife relationship, doctor and patient relationship, son-in-law and father-in-law relationship, parents and children relationship, brother and sister relationship, with special focus on father-daughter, mother-daughter and grandfather-granddaughter relationships.

The gender crisis which has given rise to identity crisis among our women folk is heart-rending when so much propaganda along with prospective marathon undertaking to strengthen women's progress has been proposed in the country's agenda. Dattani has just made the effort to highlight one of the atrocities done towards a female and belie all the hue and cry for female emancipation and equality with men on all grounds.

In *Tara*, physical deficiency has been given too much weight. Tara has been shown helpless because she has a handicap and is consequently denied the privileges of life.

But Tara could have made her deficiency, her strength and fight the society to etch a place of her own. She was a bubbly and energetic girl who had all the qualities of a normal girl. If she had been given the moral support by her parents, especially her father, she might have shone like a star as her name justifies. Her father's eager planning for her brother's future and total ignorance towards her forced her to believe that she was incompetent for any productive work. In short, her life was a burden on this earth. This made her lose interest in life altogether. Further she refuses to go to physiotherapy or fill forms for college.

Through Dattani's *Tara*, we come to know about the sincerity and inclination of a girl to prove her mettle in the world of male supremacy. As the name Tara rightfully suggests a star, the girl was a bright and shining star which was a source of cheerfulness and happiness of the family. A complete life could have done wonders and surely she would have scored the limits which her brother Chandan couldn't have. Chandan did not have the fire in him which Tara had. The character Roopa has been included in the play by Dattani to show the futility of fullness in that girl. She, though normal, was offensive and comic. Her presence makes the reader feel the waste of fullness in her and bitterness of Tara's deficiency. Tara has been depicted as a female character with potential while her brother was not enterprising at all but the father of the two was bent upon securing the future of the boy. Tara's potentiality was sacrificed on the altar of gender. Identity crisis becomes a chain with which a female is fettered when the question of choice between male and a female arises.

Dattani has been successful in hitting the target by writing the play *Tara*. He has not only focused on the futility of capacities in the girl but has also tried to show the pathetic humiliation faced by a handicap through the incident when Tara had to expose her artificial leg to the three girls in her locality. Tara is hurt and in her moment of deep hurt and resentment caused by the 'normal' world she wants to hear only Beethoven. She identifies herself with the musician with a disability who established his greatness in spite of being unable to hear his own creations. Thus, Dattani's target – gender-identity leading to identity crisis in women – has been deftly revealed in this play.

The play can be approached through the issue of simple man-woman relationship (of course unequal in our patriarchal system, like other countries), or it can be responded to in terms of the disabled children's struggle against a variety of odds, which have been put in their way by nature, or chance, or accident of their birth, or one can respond to the text through the positioning of the girl-child in Indian culture and society.

The man-woman relationship is dramatized through the interactions between Mr. Patel and his wife Bharati. He is shown to be often rude and authoritarian, when it comes to dealing with her and taking decisions. Of course, he turns out to be a caring husband, too, in his looking after Bharati during her bouts of depression. His words about Bharati reveal his concern: "Maybe I'm expecting the worst. It may never happen –no. things are getting out of hand. I must worry about her. Yes, I'm worried - about my wife" (330). But at the same time, he exhibits a streak of harshness, even heartlessness towards her. His admonition to Bharati not to give one of her kidneys to Tara who needs a kidney transplant, is not the result of his concern for his wife's health, but is the product of his cruel attitude towards her. When questioned by Bharati why he is against it, his answer is in keeping with his overall treatment of his wife:

"Because I do not want you to have the satisfaction of doing it" (344). This quite negates his professed concern which he talks about when Bharati is in the throes of depression. Similarly, he deprives Bharati of the chance to confess her sin to Tara which she has committed towards her (Tara). That would have relieved her guilt and possibly her malady, but it seems that he does not want relief for her. His words sound heartless: "No. I don't want to give her the satisfaction of confessing," (377). His summary dismissal of Bharati's opinions as inconsequential and not paying heed to her expostulations on behalf of Tara, represent him as a typical overriding patriarchal husband. It is another matter that we come to know later why Bharati was rabidly trying to champion Tara's case – it is not for the sake of Tara that she does it. It is more for herself. However, with Bharati's underlying motive for her effusions of love towards Tara becoming clear, the play does not linger on intensively on the unequal relationship between the husband and wife. This, therefore, is not the central strand, determining the progress of the plot.

The theme of odds faced by the physically challenged children (or adults) in society no doubt comes through. Tara's artificial leg, the ridicule she is subjected to by her peers at school and in the neighbourhood (by Roopa, Prema and Naline – the last two do not appear on the stage) and the limp caused by the artificial leg which symbolically serves as the marker of a disadvantage compared to others are indicative of the playwright's interest in this issue. Roopa's words about Tara are representative of the attitude of Prema and Nalini, and possibly of the society at large: "She is a real freak of nature all right" (342). But in this case too, we find that this disability does not pose an insurmountable challenge to Tara, who has the capacity to laugh at it herself, and laugh at the imbecility of those who consider it great deprivation and a subject of pity or ridicule. She is very much capable of holding her own and making the best of her life, with all its givens. This, too, therefore, does not frame the whole of the play, demanding detailed attention.

To understand the positioning of the girl-child in Indian society we can answer the question: Who has killed Tara? And why? It is not one individual who has killed Tara. It is the socio-cultural system which is responsible for her death. The beliefs, the attitudes, and the prejudices that are deep-rooted in the collective Indian cultural psyche become instrumental in taking Tara's life. It is a complex play. Issues of class and community interplay to weave the plot of the play and bring about the climactic moment of reversal of expectations. This reversal of expectations in the matter of Bharati, Tara's mother, who sympathised with Tara actually is not the central point the play makes.

Coming to the question who has killed Tara, it is proper to know who Tara is, what her background is, in what sort of family, neighbourhood and society she is born and lives and dies. She is a Siamese twin, born to the Patels – Mr. Patel (his first name is not given) and Bharati, his wife. Born conjoined as one body with her brother Chandan, she is separated by a complicated, technologically advanced surgical operation by Dr. Thakkar who is visiting India from London. The discrimination against her begins right from the process of surgery. There are three levels on which Tara is deprived of what is her due: (i) at the hands of Nature, which makes her weaker and reduces the chances of her survival. In Dr. Thakkar's words "Our greatest challenge would be to keep the girl alive. Nature wanted to kill her. We couldn't allow it." (376). (ii) At the level of the society whose attitude is reflected through her peers – her classmate in class nine, Roopa and her friends Prema and Nalini, who find amusement in her wooden leg. (iii) At the level of family, especially at the hands of her mother and maternal grandfather - they deprive her of one of the two healthy legs. Briefly going over the three levels of discrimination, we find that it is the last which would need detailed consideration:

1. Discrimination against her by nature is accidental. Generally, born as single children, girls have better chances of survival than boys. But in this case, Tara happens to be the weaker of the two twins.

2. As far as discrimination by the society is concerned, as mentioned earlier, Tara is not overly disturbed what others think of her infirmity. Therefore, it is almost insignificant.

3. Discrimination by the family is a serious matter, as it is conscious and is the result of a conspiracy against her. At the time of surgical separation from her brother, a conspiracy is hatched against her by none else than her very own mother, Bharati, who has conceived and produced her, her maternal grandfather and Dr. Thakkar. She gets deprived of one of the two healthy legs. The Siamese twins had three healthy legs. One of the healthy legs had greater chances of survival on the girl child as the blood supply to it came from the girl's body. But Tara was not given her due. She was deprived of what was hers because Bharati wanted to have a healthy and able son. So, Chandan was given the two healthy legs. This conspiracy needs to be commented upon in the light of what happens to the girl child in Indian society.

Having been successfully separated from her twin brother, her ordeal continues. It is her own mother who conspires against her. Her father, Mr. Patel, is not much different from his wife, though Bharati is guilty of a more serious crime/sin against Tara. He continuously and doggedly favours Chandan when it comes to giving him higher education abroad, and a career. (Patel: "Chandan is going to study further and he will go abroad for his higher studies". [352]). Tara is discouraged openly, not withstanding her feelings in the matter, even though she is more intelligent, sharp and witty and would perform well if given opportunities in life. It is only when Chandan refuses to go College without her, Patel thinks of sending Tara, too, to college. Bharati supports Tara in the matter of higher education and in some other cases, but her support is tainted. It is the product of the guilt and cannot be interpreted as fighting the systematic odds in Tara's way. Helena Michie's concept of "domestic carceral" is relevant here, though she has used it in a different context (in the context of women's pregnancy). She says:

The phrase 'domestic carceral' points to women's imprisonment in the home and in the marriage plot and away from teleology which seems home and marriage as benign alternatives to a world of robbers and rapists who come in from outside. (Feminisms: An Anthology of Literary Theory and Criticism, 58)

Economic and religious-cultural factors have been responsible for the antipathy against and inferiorization of the girl child. (It should be noted that this phenomenon of inferiorization of girl/woman is not peculiar to India alone). A boy helps in contributing to the family income, whether by working in the field, or elsewhere. It is through him that the *vansh* (clan) continues, because of the patriarchal system which requires the members of the family to carry caste names, coming from the father (male side). Parents can attain *moksha* only if a son does the '*kapaalkriya*' (breaking of the skull while being cremated). So either girls are killed at birth, or abandoned. The medical and technological advances have made it possible to detect the sex of the foetus. This has given an impetus to the killing of the girls, as mentioned above. All these factors combine to create the social system in which the girl child has to live and die.

Tara is killed by the social system, which controls the minds and actions of people. The trauma of coming to know the role her mother had played in her life, and the discrimination she faces at the hands of her father and grandfather become too much for her. And why is she killed? Tara is not wanted. Girls are not wanted. They are irrelevant from the points of view of religion and economics. They are dispensable.

It is noteworthy that discrimination against Tara continues even after her death. Chandan, who was always interested in writing, and who has come to England for higher studies, has transformed into Dan. He turns the story he writes into his own tragedy. It is only incidentally that he has to tell Tara's story too. Dan apologizes to Tara for doing this: "Forgive me, Tara. Forgive me for making it my tragedy" (380). It is quite another matter that it becomes Tara's tragic story also. But that is only incidental.

There are two pointers in the play which make us believe that Dattani also wants us to interpret it along the lines of the social system being the culprit in the matter of cruelty to girl children. The following conversation between Chandan and Roopa serves as a pointer:

Chandan: What would you do if you had to choose between a boy and a girl? Who would you choose?

Roopa: I think it's more civilized to drown her (girl) in milk. (365)

Chandan and Tara's maternal grandfather was a wealthy man. He was in politics and came very close to becoming the Chief Minister. His will is a testament of the kind of treatment that is meted out to girls in Indian society. Mr. Patel and Chandan are talking:

Patel: He [grandfather] left you a lot of money.

Chandan: And Tara?

Patel: Nothing.

Chandan: Why?

Patel: It was his money. He could do what he wanted with it. (360)

The worst part is that this conversation takes place in the presence of Tara. No consideration whatsoever for her feelings! Tara is the victim of this collective social system. He sums up the change he discerns in the attitude of women of yesteryear and shows how passionate they are about their daughter's independence. He reflects on their aspirations when he shows how Bharati insists that Tara and not the members of her family must decide what she wants for herself. She tells Chandan what she expects women to do these days:

BHARATI: It's time Tara decided what she wants to be. Women have to do that as well as these days. She must have a career.

CHANDAN: She can do whatever she wants. Grandfather's trust will leave us both money, isn't it?

BHARATI: Yes. But she must have something to do! She can't be – aimless all her life. (364)

The women of new generation have come out of the shadow of the old generation when they gave importance to physical beauty. Today's women give importance to intelligence and confidence because these are the qualities, which make them lead their life meaningfully and respectfully. It is this change, which makes Tara retorts when Roopa reminds her of her leg. She says that she would prefer being one-eyed, one-armed and one-legged to being an imbecile like her:

ROOPA: How dare you! You one-legged thing!

TARA: I'd sooner be one-eyed, one-armed and one-legged than be an imbecile like you. (343)

Not only that, she hates even the thought of being pitied for her physical shortcoming. She is confident of her strength, which is reflected in her reply to her father, "I am strong. My mother has made me strong." (321). She goes to the extent of saying that she does not care for the person who does not care for her. She is conscious of her self-respect and identity. Her reply to Chandan, when advised to care for people around, speaks of her strength and confidence:

CHANDAN: You should. You should care – for people around you?

TARA: How do you expect me to feel anything for anyone if they don't give me any feeling to begin with? Why is it wrong for me to be without feeling? Why are you asking me to do something that nobody has done foe me?

CHANDAN: I don't know. Somehow, it is wrong, to be so selfish.

TARA: Selfish? Yes. I am. I have the right to be selfish, like everyone else! (314)

The play presents a mirror to the Indian society to see its true face. It tries to shock the society out of its grooved thinking. Through racy dialogue and bare minimum stage-setting (by just picking out the characters though crossfadings of light) the playwright effectively portrays the interactions among the characters. The authenticity of the play is established by making Chandan (Chandu at home and later called Dan after his arrival in England) as the narrator/writer of the play. He is one of the Siamese twins and nobody could know better than he does.

Taras (stars) do not twinkle in the Indian sky because they are not allowed to.

CHAPTER THREE

Final Solutions: Issue of Communalism

Mahesh Dattani's *Final solutions* is a commendably bold play because it closely studies the communal virus which took centre stage in Indian society culminating in the Ayodhya demolition and the horrific bomb blasts in Mumbai. It has successfully highlighted the partition-related malaise, which is not just prevalent in our society until today, but fast spreading its tentacles. It raises all those questions, which either remain unresolved or have not been addressed so far. An honest effort towards actually restoring communal harmony has yet to be made. *Final solutions* bares the ugly face of communalism. It took moral courage, in the immediate aftermath of the Babri masjid nightmare, on the part of Dattani to write the play. The communal temperature nowadays is more normal. Final solutions moves from partition to present day communal tension. One community hates another. One community is the majority, the other happens to be the minority. Consequently, the two communities are at loggerheads, living in an atmosphere of conflict and acrimony. The 1990's have seen a number of films, plays and dissertations, which have tried to lift the cover off this contemporary scourge. There comes forth a reductive analysis, which reduces a complex phenomenon to a series of cause and effects. Rarely do we come across serious attempts that go beyond the superficial lesions and talk about the problem with all its complexities. Dattani looks at the socio-political problem that defies all final solutions. In Dattani's view, Hindus and Muslims are not just two cardboard communities who clash when a procession is stoned, a pooja is disrupted, a mosque is dismantled. These for him, are just the jagged tips of an ominous iceberg. One that threatens to freeze the entire landscape into polarized communities that live by intolerance and hate in place of harmony . . . more important is the iceberg – an amorphous mass that glorifies the credo of unity in diversity without actually understanding the meaning of diversity. The play looks straight into the heart of fundamentalist and the liberal and tears down the prototypes. Dattani's best play so far and as in some of his other plays, he takes the family unit as his locale and moves between the past and the present. The playwright takes three generations of a middleclass family as his base and through undercurrents that affect its members, explores the psyche of his characters in these days of communal strife. Quite a few plays have been written on the communal theme but *Final solutions* is perhaps the only one so far which, instead of moralizing and raising hollow slogans for communal harmony, examines the issue from the point of view of a sociologist and says "communal hatred is located not out on the street but deep inside ourselves," (Collected Plays 384); the play holds a mirror to the society we live in. As the dramatic tension (neatly orchestrated by a chorus) rises in the play, the subterranean psyche of each character is laid bare. Abuses are hurled, raw passions are evoked, attempts at reconciliation are made and prejudices and fears are acknowledged. The beauty of the script indeed lies in its ability to relentlessly and sensitively question. Its urgent need to use 'dialogue' as a remedy for a socially pressing issue such as communalism, is the play's underlying theme.

Final Solutions foregrounds the Hindu-Muslim problems. It also tackles the theme of transferred resentments in the context of family relations. Dattani has attempted a neat balancing act when it comes to tracing the malady of communal disharmony to certain elements within both the communities – Hindu and Muslim. The diagnosis offered is also sound enough. Paid people cause riots or politicians play upon the susceptibilities of the two communities on certain key issues. The chorus is a good device to express the broad way in which the thinking of excitable elements within the two communities goes. Processions are being taken out and then attacked and then retaliated. Somebody always is there who throws the first stone. Food habits or kitchen-fads of the two communities are brought into focus. Utensils, getting contaminated by the touch of a member of the other community, is one such fad.

Then there are resentments within the family of Ramnik Gandhi. Smita feels stifled at home.

Aruna: Does being a Hindu stifle you?

Smita: No, living with one does. (375)

Smita sees a lot wrong with the way Aruna is. Aruna's husband is also on the disapproving side. He has an exchange with Javed but neither is much wiser as a result. Bobby (Babban) tries to defuse things all the time. At a time there was something between him and Smita. Smita already knows Javed and Bobby when they seek shelter after being hounded by a mob. She knows Javed's sister Tasneem also.

She also knows what Javed does. This is the unravelling part of the plot.

The other unravelling is about the shop that got burnt down. That accounts for a guilt feeling. So self-righteousness wouldn't do. Smita feels stifled by Aruna but would not like her father to use Aruna's ways as a way of dominating her. There she is on Aruna's side. When Ramnik asks her why she didn't tell him how she felt, her reply is that she didn't want to tell him because that would have been a triumph for him over Aruna. She says: "How easy it would have been for us to join forces and make her feel she was wrong" (386).

One of the climactic scenes in the play is when Bobby touches Krishna's idol. He says that Krishna smiles at our trivial pride and trivial shows. To Javed he says, "See Javed! He doesn't humiliate you. He doesn't cringe from my touch. He welcomes the warmth of my hand" (400).

To everybody in general he says: "And if you are willing to forget, I am willing to tolerate" (400). He sees himself as a human being who believes, and tolerates, and respects what other human beings believe. The other climactic moment comes in the form of Ramnik's confession to Hardika:

It's their shop. It's the same burnt up shop we bought from them, at half its value. And we burnt it. Your husband, My father, and his father. They had burnt it in the name of communal hatred. Because we wanted a shop. (401)

The fears and anxieties of the two communities are partly an aftermath of partition. Then there is the feeling of being second grade citizens. There is the sensitivity to music being played near a mosque. There is the Hindu sensitivity in the matter of general Muslim food habits that go against vegetarianism. There are fears of contamination.

Politicians exploit most of these things. Hired goons help them. Saner voices like Bobby's are drowned, ignored or brushed aside. Pent up feelings, take a violent shape.

As far as the Ramnik Gandhi family goes, it is a lot like Pinter's play *Homecoming.* Everyone wants his/her own space but something keeps simmering. Secrets tumble out under pressure. Unconscious and conscious fears and prejudices rule. Quite a few kinds of liberalism are often only skin deep but these are needed nevertheless. Collectively a lot of healing needs to be done. Better education and greater mixing would be a part of the answer.

Critical situations bring out both our better parts and our worse parts. We can be quite cruel as a collectivity and (with the best of intentions) can be touchy for all the wrong reasons. All of us have the basest emotions hidden inside us. A demon lurks all the time. We all look for scapegoats. The false feeling of superiority is perhaps one of the worst things in such situations.

Dattani conveys all this – and more – dramatically. He allows his characters to develop. He is a dramatist endowed with a good theatre-sense and his command of language is remarkable. He often takes up tricky issues and is able to bring a lot of equanimity to his handling of these. The dialogue is mostly crisp. Character-contrasts work well. He is able to delve deep into the unconscious levels of community thinking and brings a lot of objectivity and balance to his analysis of the problems that bedevil us.

The characters in the play motivate one to think that angry outbursts lead to chain reactions. The play opens with Daksha reading from her diary. An oil lamp converted to an electric one suggests that the period is the late 1940s. Daksha is the grandmother of the Gandhis, who sometimes is seen as a girl of fifteen on the stage. Daksha thinks that she is "a young girl who does not matter to anyone outside her home" (166). She says: "Last year in August, a terrible thing happened and that was freedom for India". The Mob whispers "Freedom! At last! Freedom!" (186) Daksha closes her diary and now Hardika appears on the stage. She feels the things have not changed that much. A period of forty years is not a long period for nation. But on the stage, the drumbeat grows louder and the Chorus slowly wear the Hindu masks. The words spoken by the Chorus show the beginning of disharmony and painful period ahead. As long as the persons are on the stage, they are normal but as soon as they are behind the masks, their thirst for blood rises. Whether we are angry with someone or someone is angry with us, each outburst takes its toll on both parties. The Chorus with the Hindu masks burst with angry words:

Chorus 1: The procession has passed through these lanes

Every year, for forty years!

Chorus 2, 3: How dare they?

Chorus 1, 2, 3: For forty years our chariot has moved through

their mohallas.

Chorus 4, 5: What did they? What did they today?

Chorus 1: How dare they?

Chorus 2, 3: They broke our Rath, They broke our chariot

And felled out Gods!

Chorus 1, 2, 3: This is our land! How dare they?

Chorus 1: It is in their blood!

Chorus 2, 3: It is in their blood, to destroy!

Chorus 4: Why should they?

Chorus 5: It could have been an accident.

Chorus 2: The stone that hit our God was no accident!

Chorus 3: The knife that slit the poojari's stomach was no

accident!

Chorus 4, 5: Why should they? It could have been an accident. (168)

The works spoken by Chorus are the indications of domestic violence, political mischief and social unrest. The effective use of the Chorus in the play is a dynamic technique used by the playwright. In the stage directions, the playwright gives hints on the Mob/Chorus:

The Mob/Chorus comprises five men and ten masks on sticks. The masks are strewn all over the ramp. The player 'wears' a mask by holding the stick in front of him. At more dynamic moments, he can use it as a weapon in a stylized fashion. There are five Hindu masks and five Muslim masks. The Mob/Chorus become the Chorus when they 'wear' either the Hindu or the Muslim masks. But when once referred to individually, they remain Chorus 1, Chorus 2 etc. The players of the Mob/Chorus do not belong to any religion and ideally should wear black. (165)

"Their chariot fell in our street!" remarks Chorus 1 with Muslim masks. The words 'This is our land', 'fell in our street' show that the borderline is clear. Nobody thinks it is the land of Indians. Hardika says that the pride has destroyed her before. Her family doesn't want equality. It wants to prove that it is superior to somebody else. Hardika can't stand this 'wretched' pride game.

In the living room of the Gandhis, Aruna, Ramnik Gandhi's wife, enters while Aruna's daughter Smita and her husband are retiring for the night. Ramnik doesn't like Hardika's telling his daughter that "Those people are all demons" (173). Aruna is a typical Gujarati housewife doing 'pooja-path' everyday. She is overburdened by work. The following dialogue is a comment on the creator of the chaotic situation. When Aruna complains about her uneasiness, Ramnik asks:

Ramnik: Nobody is asking you to pray all day.

Aruna: Who do you think is protecting this house?

Ramnik: Who do you think is creating all this trouble? (173)

Aruna promises everybody: "Our Krishna will protect us. (174)

She is a God -fearing woman who thinks that everything will be smooth and peaceful one day. There is Lord Krishna who will protect everyone.

Daksha remembers her best friend Zarine. She admires her beauty: "I have never met anyone as a pretty as her! What a complexion! It's true that Khoja women are the prettiest in the whole world" (175). Daksha feels her beauty but hates the place where she lives as it is "a place where they sell unmentionable things" (175).

Ramnik saves the two boys, Bobby and Javed, when the Chorus shout: "Kill the sons of swine!" it is the demon of hate that has been let loose. Nobody helps the boys. Finally, Ramnik opens the door for the boys. The bitter hatred intensifies. The irrational behaviour of the two communities lingers for some time showing one's prowess over the other. Chorus 1, 2 shout: "We are few! But we are strong!" (179).

Chorus calls Ramnik 'a traitor' for protecting the boys. Deep hatred makes the Chorus devoid of any human feelings. Hardika betrays her feelings by saying that she hates Javed. Aruna wants that the boys must go away from the house.She gives them water but puts the empty glasses separate from the other glasses. Act I ends with the violent words of the Chorus: "Throw them out!" (187) The Chorus goes to the extent of saying: "You mad man! They'll stab you in the back! They'll rape your daughter" (186).

At the beginning of Act II, the characters are all in the same position as at the end of Act I. The Mob/Chorus is restless. The conflict deepens as the chariot lies broken in their streets. Chorus I doubts their leader's intentions. He says, "They want our blood to boil" (188). But what should boiling blood lead to, nobody knows. Chorus I laments that the leaders have succeeded in their mission after a lot of bloodshed and bitter enmity, the Chorus understand their flaw.

Smita recognizes the boys as Javed, Tasneem's brother, and Babban or Bobby, Tasneem's fiancé. Tasneem is Smita's classmate. Smita's feeling of hatred for the political parties can be traced here.

Smita : (to Ramnik) They hire him! They hire such people!

Ramnik: They who?

Smita : Those – parties! They hire him! That's how he makes a living. They bring him and many more to the city to create riots. To throw thefirst stone! (195)

Javed turns furious at these words and calls Smita a "Traitor" (195)

Act III opens with a spotlight on the two men sitting on the floor, looking troubled. The Muslim Chorus is on the highest level of the ramp. They sit with their legs folded under them in prayer position. The wordy duel between Ramnik and Javed goes on, accusing each other. The flames of hatred are still in their minds. Ramnik says to Javed that his life is based on violence. Ramnik thinks that Javed is a riot-rouser and criminal. He emits a few curses on Javed.

Ramnik thinks that Javed has done an unforgivable act. He, a liberal-minded person, offers a job to Javed only to give him a chance.

Daksha's complaint about her in-laws that they don't allow her to play gramophone makes Zarine sympathetic about Daksha. Zarine's father is busy narrating the stories about the clash between two communities and how his shop is burnt purposely. Javed sarcastically remarks: "You scream with pain and horror, but there is no one listening to you. Everyone is alone in their own cycles of joy and terror" (205). Javed admits that he himself doesn't know what he is doing there. He is totally disillusioned. Smita frankly tells her mother, Aruna, not to burden her anymore with religious prejudices.

In the last lines of the Third Act, Bobby picks up the image of Krishna and tells everybody: "He does not burn me to ashes! He does not cry out from the heavens saying He has been contaminated!" (224). Aruna feels uneasy by seeing this act but Bobby clarifies: "If you are willing to forget, I am willing to tolerate" (225).

Ramnik transfers his anger at his own father's black deed (burning the shop) to his mother. In the name of communal hatred, this shameful act is done by Ramnik's father. This is the reason why he does not want to go to his shop. In the play Smita looks very innocent. She doesn't like hypocrisy or over-reaction to religious duties. She openly opposes her mother: "I can see so clearly how wrong you are" (211). Aruna is proud of her religion. She listens to the stories of Gods while Smita thinks it is all rubbish. Aruna's own daughter does not show any respect for all the religious rituals her mother observes. Smita boldly tells her mother: "You have to admit you are wrong" (210).

We have to oust anger from our lives if we want to live peacefully. Are there any final solutions to the problem of communal riots, disputes and acts of hatred? Can we come out of this vicious circle? Mahesh Dattani gives no answer. Alyque Padamsee asks: "Is life a forward journey or do we travel round in a circle, returning to our starting point?" (161)

The play is a fine example of transferred resentments. Smita, who is unable to express her love for Babban, criticizes her mother bitterly. Smita hates praying and fasting. Her mother accuses her of running away from religion. The characters in the play express their anger at every stage. The members of the raging communities do not know that negative emotions like anger tend to release harmful toxins in the body. The mob seems to be symbolic of our own hatred. We, the people of different communities, must stop this hatred and bitterness. The play mocks at the politicians who use people as their puppets. These puppeteers are the real culprits. The playwright, at the end of the play, wishes to stop this game of hatred and communal tension through the character of Ramnik. He accepts that his father has done the black deed. We should forgive the offenders and forget the past. This can be the final solution.

CHAPTER FOUR

Conclusion

Mahesh Dattani is one of the best playwrights country has ever produced. Dattani's theatre group Playpen was formed in 1984 and he has directed several plays for them ranging from classical Greek to contemporary works. The author of more than 15 plays, he made his directorial debut with *Mango Souffle.* Over a career spanning twenty-five years he has written radio plays for the BBC and the film script of *Ek Alag Mausam* and has even had two collections of his plays published. The *International Herald Tribune* while praising Mahesh Dattani described him as "One of India's best and most serious contemporary playwrights writing in English. His own favourite playwrights as a child were Tennessee Williams and Arthur Miller. He once said "Vijay Tendulkar's *Silence! The Court is in Session* and *Sakharam Binder* impressed me with their complex portrayal of women characters" (Muffled Voices, 134).

Dattani owes his success to the fact that he had a theatre company which produced his plays and to Alyque Padamsee who spotted his talent, built it up and brought it out into the larger world of theatre in Bombay and subsequently in Delhi, Calcutta and London. Alyque Padamsee says: "At last we have a playwright who gives sixty million English-speaking Indians an identity" (Collected Plays, Cover page).

Mahesh Dattani is India's first playwright to be awarded the Sahitya Akademi Award for his contribution to the world of drama. His plays deal with religious tension, sexuality and gender issue. Alyque Padamsee calls him one of the "most serious contemporary playwrights. " He is a director, actor, dancer, teacher and writer, all rolled into one. He is a director par excellence and many of his plays have been staged to universal acclaim. He has starred in several well-known plays and has won accolades for his sterling performance in them. Dattani teaches theatre courses at the summer session programme of Portland State University, Oregon, U.S.A., and conducts workshops regularly at his studio and elsewhere. But his international acclaim rests on his writing credentials which include plays like *Where There's a Will, Tara, Bravely Fought the Queen, Final Solutions,* and *On a Muggy Night in Mumbai.* He has chronicled the social victim and the follies, foibles and prejudices of Indian society. He has criticized and exposed the Indian middle class in many of his plays. Some of his plays are eloquent defences of society's outcasts and would-be rebels people forced to live double lives in order to satisfy the prying eyes of society.

Dattani tackles issues that afflict societies the world over. Just like Ibsen and Shaw, Dattani also exposes the evils prevalent in the society. Dealing with issues like male-female ascendance divide (*Tara*), communalism (*Final solutions*), Dattani holds back nothing. He uses the world of comic theatre to encase the bitterness of the truths he is dealing with and like Bernard Shaw, Dattani also wants to use the theatre as a powerful tool for bringing about the necessary social change. Dattani excels in mirroring his society. Mahesh Dattani in an interview with Anita Nair says: "Theatre to me is a reflection of what you observe. I write plays for the sheer pleasure of communicating through this dynamic medium" (*The Plays of Mahesh Dattani*, 50)

Dattani, like his predecessors Vijay Tendulkar and Badal Sircar, believes in the fact that a playwright should write about the evils present in the society of his time and present it before the audience. For this purpose Dattani uses the medium of stage to present the problems to the audience as theatre is very close to real life. Dattani here echoes the words of Shakespeare who compared stage to the real life in Act II Scene VII of his play *As You Like It:*

All the world's a stage,

And all the men and women merely players.

They have their exits and their entrances;

And one man in his time plays many parts, (55)

His plays have varied content and varied appeal. His characters struggle for some kind of freedom and happiness under the weight of tradition, cultural construction of gender and repressed desire.

But what makes him one of India's finest playwrights is the manner in which he speaks to the audience, i.e., straight from the heart. He does not provide ready-made solution or fully resolved ending. Like Shaw, he presents the flaw before the people and in this way make people aware that such problems are a part of the society and cannot remain veiled for a long time.

On a reading of Mahesh Dattani's plays we realize that some common threads seem to be running through his plays. They reveal a vigorous mind, frantically engaged in examining and enquiring about contemporary urban issues. Central to his plays are themes like family, middle-class, gender crisis, identity crisis, homosexuality, revelation of past.

Family is his important concern. Most of Dattani's plays are woven around the stories of various families. For example, *Final Solutions* deals with the past and present of Ramnik Gandhi's family. The members of the family fight their own battles on home ground.

The middle class is his target. Dattani's plays expose the hollowness of the values and lives of middle-class people. The characters and their families put up pretence for the sake of society. They put on appearances for others and in their struggle to be successful they pay a heavy price. They are ordinary human beings, who are disillusioned with life. They are searching for happiness, love, a sense of belonging and even sexual satisfaction. They strive to achieve all this within the framework of the family.

Gender identity is another theme. One recurring theme in Dattani's plays is the role of men and women in society, or the preconceived notion of genders. His plays point out that we have pre-defined ideas about what constitutes masculinity or femininity. Society has fixed norms about how men and women ought to behave. Dattani's plays seem to challenge these fixed notions. Dattani questions gender stereotypes. Defining new gender roles and traits is an important theme of Dattani's play.

The emergence of new woman and clash of values have an important place. Dattani's women are brave and assertive; be it Baa, Dolly or Alka of *Bravely Fought the Queen*; Tara of *Tara*; Kiran of *Where There's a Will*; Ratna of *Dance Like a Man*; all of them are "new" women, bold and self confident. They have well defined concept of their existence and are conscious of their identities. He also reflects on the clash of values and generation gap in his plays.

Discrimination against the girl child is handled boldly by Dattani in his play, *Tara*. The play deals with the courage and strong will of a handicapped Siamese twin who could have survived but for her mother's unwise and preferential decision to give up the extra leg to her twin brother, Chandan. Gender identity is yet another theme that dominates the plays of Mahesh Dattani.

Final solutions is a play outwardly focused on Hindu–Muslim incompatibility but inwardly full of mutual disagreements amongst the family members. The clash between fanaticism of Hindus versus fanaticism of Muslims is highlighted. Lack of accommodation between the two communities and unacceptability gives rise to acrimony resulting in terrorism and anarchy. The play itself is a question mark on the age – old enmity between the two communities wondering if there would ever be a final solution to this endemic problem.

Dattani reflects on the predicament of women in the past, comments on their status in the present, dramatizes his understanding of who he considers responsible for their predicament and exhorts us to shed our age-old prejudices in order to have peace and harmony in family and society. There was a time when women accepted unhesitatingly the dos and don'ts men decided for them but Tara refuses to accept that somebody else should decide for them. She asserts her independence and wants to shape her life and priorities the way she considers proper.

He reflects in its wake on the status of women in society and the attitude of women manning the kitchen, the existing dowry system that spells doom for girls and the difference in the attitudes of girls belonging to two different classes, the attitude of modern educated girls and the discrimination perpetrated against women, the activities man has earmarked for women, and the concept of equality that is gaining ground, a woman's unethical preference for a male child and the status of a married man in a family that allows the in-laws to interfere and decide for them, the difference in the attitudes of two generations to women and the emergence of career women in society, the qualities of women which they have to learn to use for the proper growth of society and human being and his understanding of how love ensures domestic peace and happiness.

Summing up, Dattani's plays are noted for dealing with common place but extremely relevant and contemporary themes. He has the courage to discuss unconventional themes like homosexuality, men pursuing dance as career, pain and suffering of conjoined twins and child sexual abuse. The marginalized and the invisible in the society are his priority. It is the conflicts and frictions that arise from patriarchy, religious intolerance, gender and sexuality that he tries to explore in-depth through his plays. As the family units form the microcosm of this conflicting contemporary world in the plays of Mahesh Dattani, they are projected as seething cauldrons of emotional turmoil that come to a boil and spill over, when a tinder of turbulence is introduced unwittingly, underneath.

CHAPTER FIVE

Works Cited

Dattani, Mahesh. *Collected Plays*. New Delhi: Penguin, 2000.

- - -. *Contemporary Indian Theatre and Its Relevance: Journal of Indian Writing in English*. Vol 30, Jan 2002.

Gupt, Bharat. *Dramatic Concepts: Greek and Indian*. New Delhi: D. K. Print World, 1944.

Iyengar, K.R.S. *Drama in Modern India*. Bombay: The P.E.N. All India Centre, 1961.

- - -. *Indian Writing in English*. Bombay: Asia, 1977.

Kriplani, Krishna. *Literature of Modern India*. New Delhi: National Book Trust, 1982.

Kumar, Satish. *A Survey of Indian English Drama*. Bareilly: Prakash Book Depot, 2004.

Misra, Manoj Kumar. *A Study of Mahesh Dattani's Tara*. New Delhi: Swarup and Sons, 2005.

Naik, M.K. *The Achievement of Indian Drama in English*. New Delhi: Sterling, 1984.

Padamsee, Alyque. *A Note on the play Final Solutions:Collected Plays*. New Delhi: Penguin, 2000.

Prasad, A.N. *Studies in Indian Drama in English*. Bareilly: Prakash Book Depot, 2004.

Rengacharya, Aditya. *The NatyaSastra*. Eng. Translation, New Delhi: Munshiram Manohar Lal, 1996.

Shakespeare, William. *As You Like It*. Ed. Agnes Latham. London: Methuen, 1975.

Nair, Anita. "Mahesh Dattani: The Invisible Observer." *Anita Nair: The Official Website* (May 2001) 3pp April 2011
<http:www.anitanair.net/pages/profiles-md.htm>
<http:www.indianexpress.com/bangalore/expression/readers html.>
<http:www.maheshdattani.com.>

Printed by Libri Plureos GmbH in Hamburg, Germany